HOW TO KNOW YOU'RE MISMANAGING YOUR FINANCES; 21

Proven Steps To Regain Financial Control

Leticia D. O'Neil

Table of Contents

Introduction

It is all too simple to slip into the trap of mismanaging our funds in a society filled with alluring commercials, cultural pressures, and the relentless quest for material items. Many people frequently make unintentional financial blunders that might have a negative influence on their present and future well-being.

The thorough manual "How to Know You're Mismanaging Your Finances" illuminates the typical traps and errors that people frequently make when navigating their financial lives. The goal of this book is to provide readers with the information and skills they need to identify and correct these errors, ultimately paving the road to a path of financial wellness.

This book will be your dependable companion whether you're a young professional just starting your career, an experienced adult making difficult financial decisions, or someone looking to take back control of their finances. It offers useful information, suggestions for action, and examples from real life that will appeal to readers from all walks of life.

You will discover how to recognize the red flags that suggest you could be mismanaging your funds as you go through the pages below. This book explores the fundamental problems that can undermine your financial security, such as excessive spending, forgoing savings, piling up high-interest debt, and failing to make long-term plans. You may proactively adjust your course and take control of your financial situation by being aware of these mistakes.

Furthermore, "How to Know You're Mismanaging Your Finances" doesn't simply concentrate on the issues; it also offers practical solutions and tried-and-true methods to deal with them. You will learn the value of creating a budget, setting aside money for unplanned expenses, investing properly, and developing sound money management practices. By following these guidelines, you can take back control of your money, lessen stress, and lay the groundwork for a profitable future. Remember, you can achieve financial security; the first step is to identify and correct any mistakes you may have made in the past.

So come along with me on this instructive voyage of financial and self-discovery. Let's identify the frequent errors that frequently go unreported and set out on a route to monetary stability and independence. We will find the solutions together so you may reach your financial potential and build a better future yourself for you and your loved ones.

Chapter 1

FINANCIAL MANAGEMENT

How do you handle your finances?

The practice of managing your money responsibly and efficiently is referred to as money management. It encompasses several techniques and tactics aimed at making the most of your money's potential and usage, maintaining financial stability, and attaining your financial objectives. The fundamental components of effective money management are

- Budgeting: This is a crucial aspect of financial management. It entails keeping track of your income and spending, allocating money for various needs including housing, transportation, groceries, entertainment, and savings, and ensuring that your expenses and income are in balance.

- Saving: Money management stresses the significance of setting aside some of your money for upcoming requirements and unexpected expenses. Setting financial objectives, creating an emergency fund, and forming thrifty spending and automated savings deductions are all part of it.

- Investing: Managing your money means choosing wisely where to put your money to build your wealth over time. Depending on your level of risk tolerance and your financial goals, this may entail investing in stocks, bonds, real estate, mutual funds, or other investment vehicles.

- Debt management: Taking care of your debt is essential for sound money management. It entails comprehending and managing your debt, paying bills on time, and avoiding high-interest obligations. To efficiently manage and lower debt, strategies including debt consolidation, refinancing, and setting repayment priorities can be used.

- Risk management: Managing money also entails identifying and reducing financial risks. This entails getting life, health, and property insurance, as well as making a contingency plan for unforeseen circumstances. Risk management shields your financial stability from unanticipated events.

Overall, managing your finances holistically is what money management entails. To get the most out of your money and safeguard your financial future, you need discipline, preparation, and educated decision-making.

The Value Of Financial Management

Money management is crucial for several reasons:

1. Financial Stability: Prudent financial management contributes to achieving and preserving financial stability. You can prevent living paycheck to paycheck and lower your chance of going into debt by making a budget, keeping track of your spending, and conserving money. It offers a strong basis for taking care of financial commitments, handling crises, and reaching financial objectives.

2. Goal Achievement: Good money management gives you the power to

define and meet financial objectives. Effective money management enables you to direct resources toward certain goals, whether they are saving for a down payment on a home, paying for your child's school, starting a business, or making retirement plans. It assists you in staying on course, monitoring your progress, and making any required corrections as you go.

3. Sound Financial Management techniques help with debt management and debt reduction. You may prevent taking on too much debt and strive towards becoming debt-free by making a budget and giving debt payback priority. To reduce interest costs and raise your credit score, it aids in helping you comprehend your financial commitments, work out payment

arrangements, and make on-time payments.

4. Financial Independence and Flexibility: Using money management gives you the independence and flexibility to make decisions based on your financial priorities. Making good financial decisions can give you greater control over your resources and will allow you to decide whether to spend, save or invest. As a result, you can take measured risks, seize chances and feel more financially secure.

5. Emergency Preparedness: Unexpected events might negatively affect your financial situation. Building an emergency fund, which serves as a safety net against unforeseen circumstances like job loss, medical costs, or home repairs, is made easier

with good money management. Having a safety net lowers stress and the need to use expensive credit cards or loans to cover unexpected expenses.

6. Better Financial Relationships: Good money management enhances your connections with creditors, lenders, and financial organizations. You may get better loan conditions, cheaper interest rates, and greater credit limits by practicing effective money management, paying your bills on time, and maintaining a strong credit score. It improves your financial standing and makes good financial prospects more accessible.

7. Building Wealth: Good money management is essential to long-term wealth development. You may increase your assets and establish a solid

financial foundation by prudently
saving and investing. Your money may
work for you and create returns by
being invested in a variety of assets,
including stocks, bonds, real estate, and
retirement accounts, assisting you in
building wealth and achieving financial
independence.

8. Reduced Financial Worry: Anxiety and
   worry related to money are frequently
   caused by poor money management.
   Financial stress and concerns may be
   reduced by actively managing your
   money, making a budget, and living
   within your means. The dread of
   financial uncertainty is lessened by a
   well-structured financial plan, which
   also fosters general well-being.

9. Better Decision-Making: Good money
   management practices disciplined and

knowledgeable decision-making. You become more capable of making wise financial decisions when you carefully monitor your income and spending, consider your financial objectives, and weigh the benefits and dangers of different financial options. This is true for daily financial decisions such as spending, saving, investing, and managing debt.

10. Financial Education and Awareness: Using sound money management techniques helps you become more financially literate and aware. You develop financial literacy by keeping a close eye on your accounts, looking into investment options, and keeping up with personal finance issues. You may use this information to protect yourself from financial abuse, identify

possible frauds, and make
well-informed decisions.

11.   Planning for Your Future: Using
sound financial management, you may
make plans for the future and leave a
financial legacy for your loved ones.
You may make certain that your fortune
is transferred with your preferences by
carefully managing your assets, setting
up trusts, and developing a thorough
estate plan. Making arrangements for
future generations and protecting your
assets are both aided by good money
management.

12.   Better Quality of Life: In the end,
wise financial management helps
people live happier, more fulfilling
lives. It enables the ability to follow
your passions, hobbies, and
experiences without ongoing financial

worries, lowers stress, and provides financial security. You may better connect your financial resources with your beliefs and goals by practicing sound money management, which will increase your level of life happiness.

Why Is Financial Mismanagement Identification Important?

Finding your financial mistakes is important for various reasons:

1. Financial health awareness: Acknowledging financial mismanagement gives you a clear picture of your financial status. It assists you in determining whether you are spending too much, building debt, or not saving enough money. Making educated judgments and taking remedial actions is difficult without this insight.

2. Limiting additional harm: Limiting further harm to your financial well-being can be achieved by early detection of financial mismanagement. You may intervene and take action to lessen the damage by identifying patterns of excessive spending, excessive debt, or bad investment decisions.

3. Chance for course correction: Once financial malfeasance is discovered, there is a chance for change. To find opportunities for improvement, you might assess your spending patterns, budgeting procedures, and financial objectives. This can entail changing your way of life, cutting back on wasteful spending, or getting help from a professional to take back control of your money.

4. Debt management and repayment: Poor money management frequently causes debt to accumulate. You can create a debt management strategy to methodically pay off

outstanding debts by determining the areas of mismanagement. This can entail haggling with lenders, reorganizing debt, or enlisting the aid of credit counseling organizations.

5. Establishing a solid financial foundation: You may establish the groundwork for a more secure financial future by addressing financial mismanagement. You may strengthen your financial position and work towards attaining your financial objectives by changing negative financial habits, creating a budget, and using responsible money management techniques.

6. Avoiding financial stress and anxiety: Stress and worry are sometimes brought on by poor money management. You may lessen financial stress and restore control over your finances by recognizing and correcting the mismanagement. Your physical and mental health will both increase as a result.

7. Long-term financial security: Securing your long-term financial future requires recognizing financial mismanagement. You may strive toward financial stability, amass savings, make prudent investments, and prepare for retirement by resolving any concerns that already exist and establishing sound financial practices. An improved future is made possible by this proactive attitude.

8. Better decision-making: Being aware of financial mismanagement enables you to make more smart and knowledgeable financial choices. You can prioritize your spending and make adjustments depending on your financial objectives when you know where your money is going and how it is being mishandled. Long-term, this results in improved decision-making and more positive outcomes.

9. Better financial literacy: Identifying financial mismanagement gives you the chance to become more financially literate. You may educate yourself on personal financial subjects like budgeting, saving, investing, and debt management as you go deeper into understanding the underlying causes of mismanagement. You now possess the knowledge and abilities required to go forward and make more informed financial decisions.

10. Fraud and scam protection: Poor financial management might increase your susceptibility to fraud and scams. You become more watchful and better able to defend yourself against financial scammers by recognizing and resolving any mismanagement concerns. You'll be able to see red flags, engage in responsible financial habits, and protect your financial assets.

11. Improved relationships and communication: Poor money management can cause interpersonal problems, especially when there are shared expenses or obligations. You create opportunities for open dialogue and teamwork by recognizing and dealing with these problems. This enables you to establish a common knowledge of your financial goals and identify ways to enhance your financial management with your spouse, family, or financial adviser.

12. Goal-setting and future planning: Determining financial mismanagement enables you to evaluate your present financial situation and pinpoint areas that require improvement. You may then use this information to make financial objectives for the future that are both attainable and reasonable. Understanding your financial mismanagement gives you the power to

match your objectives with your resources and create a strategy to achieve them, whether you're saving for a down payment, establishing a company, or planning for retirement.

13. Financial tranquility: Managing your money poorly can lead to worry, anxiety, and uncertainty about your financial future. You may reclaim your mental well-being by recognizing and treating these problems. Having control over your finances and implementing adjustments that will lead to financial stability gives you a sense of security and lessens the emotional toll that comes with financial mismanagement.

Remember that spotting financial mismanagement is not about assigning blame or passing judgment, but rather about accepting responsibility and taking proactive measures to remedy any difficulties. It's an essential step to achieving financial security because it enables you to make wise decisions, guard against financial dangers, and move toward a more secure and successful future.

Chapter 2

Financial Management Fundamentals

The foundations of financial management are a collection of guidelines for people and businesses on how to manage their resources successfully. These foundational ideas include:

- ☐ Financial Planning: Setting financial objectives, formulating a strategy to get there, and coming up with tactics to allocate resources wisely are all part of financial planning. It entails evaluating the existing state of affairs financially, forecasting future earnings and outlays, and formulating a strategy to maximize cash flow.

- [ ] The act of developing a thorough plan for how money will be earned and spent is known as budgeting. To make ensuring that expenditure complies with financial objectives, requires tracking revenue, outlays, and savings. Prioritizing costs, locating potential cost-saving measures, and keeping track of financial progress are all made easier with a budget.

- [ ] Monitoring and maximizing the inflow and outflow of cash from a person's or an organization's accounts is the focus of cash flow management. To preserve liquidity, pay expenses, and ensure financial stability, it entails properly managing income, spending, and investments.

- [ ] Risk management entails locating and reducing possible monetary hazards.

Assessing and managing risks associated with investments, insurance coverage, legal and regulatory compliance, and unanticipated occurrences are all part of it. Strategies for risk management are designed to reduce possible losses and safeguard assets.

☐ Investment Management: The process of selecting investments to maximize returns while taking risk tolerance into account is referred to as investment management. It entails locating appropriate investment possibilities, carrying out research and analysis, diversifying investments, and keeping an eye on performance. Growth of wealth and attainment of financial objectives are aided by effective investment management.

☐ Debt management: Debt management
aims to manage and reduce debt
efficiently. It entails comprehending
and keeping track of debt levels, paying
bills on time, and devising plans to cut
back on or pay off high-interest debt. A
healthy debt-to-income ratio is
maintained and overall financial health
is improved through debt management.

☐ Financial Reporting and Analysis:
Using financial statements and key
performance indicators, financial
reporting and analysis involves
monitoring and assessing a company's
financial performance. It aids in
determining a person's or an
organization's financial stability,
profitability, and effectiveness.
Decision-making may be aided by
financial analysis, which also allows
for course adjustment when necessary.

☐ Tax planning entails reducing tax liabilities while adhering to all relevant tax rules and regulations. It involves comprehending tax exemptions, credits, and deductions; making tax efficient, and applying tax planning techniques to increase revenue after taxes.

☐ Financial Literacy: The cornerstone of efficient money management is financial literacy. This includes learning about and comprehending financial theories, instruments, and tactics. Enhancing financial literacy enables people to manage their personal or organizational money efficiently, make educated financial decisions, and protect themselves from fraud or scams.

You may create a strong basis for good financial management, accomplish financial objectives, and create long-term financial success by sticking to these principles.

Chapter 3

Red Flags of Poor Financial Management

The warning signs or indicators that point to inappropriate handling or financial manipulation in an organization's or an individual's financial affairs are known as red flags of financial mismanagement. Here are some typical red signs to look out for, however, they may vary based on the situation:

1. Spending above Your Means: Consistently living over your means and regularly exceeding your income raises serious warning flags. It implies a lack of financial planning and self-discipline that may result in rising debt and unstable finances.

2. Frequent Late Payments: Missing deadlines for payments, paying bills, loans, or credit cards beyond the due date, and accruing late penalties are all indications of bad money management. It shows a lack of planning and poor cash flow management, which might result in ruined credit and more financial stress.

3. Excessive Debt: Having a lot of debt, especially if it keeps rising, might be a warning sign. It could be a sign of borrowing above your means, racking up high-interest debt, or being unable to successfully manage and pay off debt.

4. Lack of Savings: It indicates bad money management if you continuously struggle to save money or have little to no savings. You may be

more susceptible to financial problems and have less financial security if you don't establish an emergency fund or save money for your future objectives.

5. Over-reliance on Credit: Using credit cards frequently to pay regular bills or to make ends meet may be a sign of poor money management. It shows an inability to efficiently manage cash flow and might lead to the accumulation of significant credit card debt.

6. Ignoring Financial Statements: It's a warning sign when someone neglects to read and comprehend financial statements, such as bank or investment statements or credit card statements. It suggests that you are not aware of or involved in your financial condition,

which makes it challenging to see possible problems or possibilities.

7. Lack of Financial Planning or Goals: Lack of financial planning or goal-setting is an indicator of bad money management. Making educated financial decisions and prioritizing spending and saving becomes difficult without a defined set of goals and a plan.

8. Hiding Financial Information: Refusing to talk about money with partners, family members, or financial experts might be a warning sign. It could be a sign of poor money management, impending concerns, or a refusal to deal with money problems.

9. Poor Retirement Planning: A lack of retirement savings and planning is an

indication of poor money management. Failure to plan for retirement may result in insufficient cash in the future and financial hardships during retirement.

10.   Lack of Insurance Coverage: You may be financially exposed if you lack insurance coverage or fail to keep up with essential policies like health, property, or life insurance. In the event of unforeseen circumstances or emergencies, it may lead to substantial financial losses and implies a lack of risk management.

11.   Lack of Financial Documentation: Failure to keep track of crucial financial records, like tax returns, investment statements, and loan agreements, may suggest disarray and possible problems with financial

management. Missed chances or
trouble keeping track of and managing
your finances might result.

It is crucial to remember that exhibiting one
or two of these warning signs does not imply
that there is financial mismanagement going
on. But if you detect repeated red flags or
trends over time, it can be a sign that you
need to evaluate and strengthen your
financial management procedures. A
financial adviser may provide expert
guidance in identifying and resolving these
problems.

Chapter 4

Recognizing Money Mindsets and Behaviors

Money psychology

This is a reference to how people feel about money and their attitudes, behaviors, and ideas about it. It looks at how our attitudes toward money might affect the choices we make and the way we act about money. The psychology of money can be summarized in the following ways:

1. Money Scripts: Our unconscious thoughts and presumptions about money influence how we behave financially. Our attitudes about earning, spending, saving, and investing may be influenced by these scripts, which are frequently created in infancy. Some examples of money scripts include "Money is the root of all evil" and "More

money will make me happy." Understanding and maybe challenging harmful attitudes can be accomplished by becoming aware of our money scripts.

2. Emotional Attachments: Strong feelings like fear, worry, happiness, or security can be triggered by money. Our ability to make decisions can be impacted by our emotional connections to money. For instance, the need for rapid satisfaction may be the driving force behind impulsive spending, while fear of financial uncertainty may result in hoarding or excessive saving. Making wise financial decisions requires understanding and controlling our emotional reactions to money.

3. Cognitive Biases: Cognitive biases can affect how we make financial decisions. There are several common biases, such as anchoring (heavily depending on prior information when making decisions), loss

aversion (fearing losses more than appreciating wins), and confirmation bias (seeking information that supports our previous ideas). Making more sensible and unbiased financial decisions can be facilitated by being aware of these biases.

4. Setting Specific Financial Objectives: Having specific financial objectives will help with motivation and direction. Goals might be short-term, like paying off debt, medium-term, like saving for a down payment, or long-term, like planning for retirement. Making decisions that promote our financial well-being is made easier when our objectives, values, and priorities are in alignment.

5. Financial Confidence and Self-Efficacy: Our attitudes toward our capacity to handle money wisely have an impact on our financial actions. We may be empowered to

make wise decisions, take measured chances, and persevere in the face of difficulties if we feel self-assured and effective in managing our finances. Increasing financial confidence is a result of developing one's financial knowledge and abilities.

6. Social and Cultural Influences: Social and cultural variables can have an impact on how we see money. Our connection with money can be influenced by a variety of factors, including cultural values, peer pressure, and societal conventions. Understanding these variables can aid us in assessing their effects and making decisions that are in line with our financial objectives and beliefs.

7. Money and Happiness: There is a complicated connection between money and happiness. Even if having enough money to cover basic expenses and provide security is essential, research indicates that, after you

pass a certain point, having more money does not always translate into being happier. Finding a balance between money and other parts of life, such as relationships and personal fulfillment, is essential. Financial well-being should be prioritized.

We may better understand our financial attitudes, habits, and prejudices by being more aware of the psychology of money. We may increase our overall financial well-being and make more wise decisions that are in line with our long-term objectives by addressing limiting beliefs, controlling emotions, and forming good financial habits.

Unhealthy monetary attitudes and practices

Financial well-being can be hampered and negatively affected by unsound money attitudes and actions. Here are some illustrations:

1. Constantly spending more than you make, using credit cards for regular costs, and making impulsive purchases without thinking about the long-term effects might result in financial distress and debt buildup.

2. Living over your means: This can result in a cycle of debt and financial instability. Adopting a lifestyle that surpasses your income and depending on loans or other forms of support to maintain it can also be a problem.

3. Financial Denial or Avoidance: Ignoring or ignoring financial issues like unpaid bills, growing debt, or a lack of funds can make matters worse and keep you from taking proactive measures to make things better.

4. Hoarding or Scarcity Mindset: Excessive savings and a refusal to spend money even when required, motivated by a lack of mentality or fear of scarcity, can limit prospects for development and investment and hinder you from reaping the rewards of your financial resources.

5. Jealousy and Comparison: Constantly comparing oneself to others and experiencing jealousy or a sense of inadequacy due to material things or apparent prosperity can result in excessive spending, debt, and discontentment with one's financial condition.

6. Financial Dependence: Reliance on others for financial assistance without making an effort to achieve financial independence might impede personal development and self-sufficiency.

7. Skipping Financial Planning: Skipping financial planning can lead to a lack of direction, lost opportunities, and challenges in reaching long-term financial stability. Setting financial objectives, making a budget, and planning for the future can all help avoid these problems.

8. Procrastination and Inaction: Postponing key financial chores like timely bill payment, debt relief, or future investment can hurt your finances in the form of late fees, penalties, missed chances, or a lack of financial preparation.

9. Excessive Risk-Taking: Making high-risk investments or engaging in speculative activities without conducting adequate research, comprehension, or diversification can result in substantial losses and financial instability.

10. Financial Dishonesty and Secrets: Hiding financial information, lying about money, or participating in financial adultery can erode confidence, lead to arguments, and obstruct honest discussion of financial objectives and difficulties.

It's critical to acknowledge these negative financial attitudes and habits and take action to change them. To break these bad behaviors and advance financial well-being, it might be helpful to seek expert advice when necessary, learn better financial habits, set realistic objectives, and seek financial education.

Typical financial blunders

People frequently make several typical financial blunders. Here are a few examples:

1. Overspending and living beyond one's means: It's a regular error to spend more than

one makes. It can result in financial stress, debt, and the inability to put money aside for the future.

2. Not budgeting: It might be challenging to successfully manage your finances if you don't set up and adhere to a budget. It's simple to overspend or lose sight of where your money is going without a budget.

3. Forgetting to save for emergencies: Many individuals forget how crucial it is to have an emergency fund. Without savings, you might have to rely on credit cards or loans to cover unforeseen costs like medical bills or auto repairs.

4. Building up high-interest debt: Using credit cards or loans with high-interest rates frequently might result in a debt cycle. To avoid paying a lot of interest, it's critical to

manage your debt and pay it off as quickly as you can.

5. Not investing for retirement: Postponing or putting off retirement savings might have long-term repercussions. Early retirement planning and persistent saving will help your money grow over time and give you a buffer for your elderly years.

6. Ignoring investments and not diversifying: Putting all of your money into one investment or not investing at all will restrict your ability to increase your wealth. Your chances of reaching long-term financial goals are increased and risk is spread out with the aid of investment diversification.

7. Lack of sufficient insurance protection: If you don't have the right insurance protection, such as health insurance, vehicle insurance, or homeowner's insurance, you might suffer

severe financial losses in the event of unforeseen events.

8. Impulsive financial choices: Making snap judgments without carefully weighing the repercussions might have unfavorable financial effects. Before making big financial decisions, it's crucial to take your time, do your homework, and consult a professional.

9. Ignoring financial education: Financial illiteracy might limit your capacity to make wise financial judgments. You may improve your financial decisions by learning more about personal finance and consulting with financial experts.

10. Neglecting to routinely evaluate and modify financial plans: As life circumstances change, it's important to periodically examine and modify your financial plans. Missed chances or financial challenges may result

from a failure to adjust to changing circumstances.

11. Forgetting to keep track of expenses: If you don't keep track of your spending, it may be challenging to find places where you may make cuts or save money. By regularly keeping an eye on your expenditure, you can maintain accountability and make the required corrections.

12. Spending impulsively without taking into account how it would affect your long-term financial objectives might jeopardize your capacity to maintain financial security. Make sure to distinguish between needs and wants while making financial decisions.

13. Ignoring credit score and credit report: If you don't frequently check your credit report and watch your credit score, you risk missing errors or even identity theft. Your ability to

obtain loans or preferable interest rates may also be impacted by having a low credit score.

14. Accepting the initial price offered without trying to haggle or look about for better prices. This is a common mistake. Long-term savings can be achieved by taking the time to compare costs, bargain for cheaper pricing, or look for special offers.

15. Overdependence on one source of income: If your only source of income, such as your work, is disrupted, you may be at risk of facing financial difficulties. Greater financial security and flexibility can be achieved by developing numerous sources of income.

16. Lack of estate planning: Not establishing an estate plan or writing a will might result in issues and disagreements over how to divide

your assets. It's critical to make plans for the future to protect your loved ones in the case of your demise.

17. Under-utilizing employee benefits: Many employees fail to make use of the employee benefits that are provided by their companies, such as health savings accounts, retirement plans, and assistance programs. Utilizing these advantages can offer important financial resources and help.

18. Trying to maintain a particular lifestyle or follow other people's spending patterns might result in excessive expenditure and financial distress. It's crucial to concentrate on your financial objectives and put your demands before those of society.

19. Timing the market: Attempting to forecast market changes and basing investing choices on transient patterns can be

dangerous. It is difficult to time the market perfectly constantly, and attempting to do so may lead to lost chances or losses.

20. Ignoring self-care and wellness: Neglecting your physical and emotional health can have a negative financial impact. In the long term, neglecting your health might affect your capacity to maintain your financial security due to medical costs or lost productivity.

You can make better decisions, give your financial health a top priority, and work toward reaching your long-term financial objectives by avoiding these frequent financial blunders.

Chapter 5

Methods for determining your present financial condition

You may use a variety of techniques and analyze important parts of your money to evaluate your present financial condition. Following are some practical methods for assessing your financial situation:

- Calculate Net Worth: To calculate your net worth, deduct your assets (cash, investments, property, etc.) from your liabilities (debts and financial commitments). This estimate gives you a broad overview of your financial situation.

- Review Revenue and Expenses: Examine your sources of revenue and keep track of your outgoing costs for a given time frame, such as a month or a year. Organize your spending into categories to see how your money is being used and determine whether your income is enough to pay for your costs.

- Analyze your current debts, including credit card debt, loans, mortgages, and student loans, to determine your current debt levels. Find out the total amount outstanding, the interest rate, and the minimum payment due, and assess your capacity to manage and pay off the obligations.

- Assess your emergency fund and savings accounts. Evaluate them both. Calculate your savings to see if it will be enough to cover emergencies or unforeseen costs. If your savings rate is in line with your financial objectives, take this into account.

- Review Investment Portfolios and Retirement Accounts: Examine your investment holdings, which may include equities, bonds, mutual funds, and retirement accounts like 401(k) or IRAs. Determine whether the performance of your assets is in line with your risk appetite and long-term objectives by evaluating how they have performed.

- Examine Insurance Coverage: Consider the details of your various insurance contracts, including those for health, life, disability, and property. Make sure you and your assets are sufficiently protected by the coverage and premiums by evaluating them.

- Check Credit Report: Request a copy of your credit report from one of the credit agencies and look over it to see your credit history, unpaid bills, and credit score. You may take the necessary steps to fix any mistakes or inconsistencies and raise your creditworthiness by recognizing them.

- Take into account your long-term and short-term financial goals while planning your finances. Determine the objectives you have in mind, like buying a home, launching a company, or setting aside money for retirement. Consider if your present financial condition supports those goals and what activities you need to take to accomplish them.

- Review Financial Statements: Collect and go through your bank statements, credit card statements, investment account statements, and any other financial statements you may have.

Understand your cash flow, spending habits, and investment returns by analyzing your income, costs, and investment performance.

- Track Your Cash Flow: Organize and routinely check your income and outgoings to track your cash flow. This enables you to see where your money is going, pinpoint areas where you can cut down or save, and make modifications to line your spending with your financial objectives.

- Debt-to-Income Ratio Calculation: To get your debt-to-income ratio, divide your gross monthly income by the sum of all your monthly debt payments. This ratio reveals how much debt you have about your income and aids in figuring out whether your income and

debt commitments are in a healthy
balance.

- Analyze different financial parameters
to have a better understanding of your
financial situation. For instance, the
debt ratio (total debt divided by total
assets) reveals the percentage of your
assets that are financed by debt, while
the savings ratio (savings divided by
income) shows how much of your
income you are saving.

- Assess Financial Risks: Consider the
dangers posed by your current financial
status. Think about potential risks like
losing your work, having health
problems, or having property damaged,
and consider how prepared you are to
address those risks. To reduce financial
risks, review your insurance coverage,

emergency savings, and contingency plans.

- Review Tax condition: Examine your tax returns, deductions, and any prospective tax advantages or obligations to determine your current tax condition. Think about whether you are utilizing all the available tax benefits and get advice from a tax expert if necessary.

- Assess Your Work and Income Potential: Consider your present work path, income potential, and room for progress. Think about if you are happy with your present level of income and whether there are any opportunities to increase it through education, skill development, or job changes.

Last but not least, consider receiving expert advice from a financial counselor or planner if you feel overwhelmed or hesitant about evaluating your financial status. They may offer unbiased advice, aid in the interpretation of financial data, and help you create a unique financial strategy. Remember that when circumstances change over time, it is critical to routinely analyze and reassess your financial condition. It enables you to see problem areas, make the required corrections, and continue working toward your financial objectives.

Chapter 6

Effects of financial mismanagement

Financial well-being can be significantly impacted by poor money management. However, the following are some typical effects of poor money management:

1. Excessive Debt: Bad financial planning frequently results in excessive debt. This might happen as a result of excessive spending, the use of credit cards with high-interest rates, taking out loans without thinking about the ability to pay them back, or ineffective budgeting. Financial stress, large interest payments, and a lack of financial flexibility can all be caused by excessive debt.

2. Constant Financial Hardship: Poor money management might result in ongoing financial hardship. Living paycheck to

paycheck, finding it difficult to pay for necessities, or worrying about bills all the time can be damaging to one's mental and emotional health. Relationships, work performance, and general quality of life can all be impacted by financial stress.

3. Inability to Save and Invest: People who handle their money poorly frequently are unable to save and invest wisely. Missed opportunities for wealth growth and financial stability can occur from failing to prioritize saving or ignoring long-term financial goals. It becomes challenging to manage unforeseen costs, accumulate an emergency fund, or prepare for retirement without savings or investments.

4. Living Above Your Means: Living above your means is a result of poor money management. This involves living over one's means, relying extensively on credit, or

borrowing frequently to support a lifestyle that is not long-term sustainable. Living above one's means can cause financial instability, debt accumulation, and difficulty supplying basic requirements.

5. Limited Financial Possibilities: Poor money management frequently restricts a person's financial possibilities. It is more difficult to get loans, get good interest rates, or access financial goods and services if you have a bad credit score or a history of financial mismanagement. Opportunities for advancement, including getting a home, establishing a company, or going to school, might be limited by a lack of financial resources.

6. Missed Investment Chances: People may overlook worthwhile investment chances as a result of poor money management. Saving and investing poorly can lead to missed

opportunities for returns and slower wealth creation over time. Without sound financial planning and investing strategies, people risk missing out on opportunities to increase their wealth and meet long-term financial objectives.

7. Retirement Insecurity: One typical result of poor money management is failing to plan and save for retirement. People who don't have enough saved for retirement risk having financial difficulties as they age. Only relying on government assistance or family support may not be enough to maintain the desired standard of living in retirement.

8. General Financial Instability: Poor financial management might result in a lack of stability. People are more vulnerable to financial crises, such as job loss, medical problems, or economic downturns, if they lack appropriate money management

abilities. Unexpected failures can interrupt a person's life and make it difficult to bounce back.

9. A damaged Credit Score: Bad financial management frequently results in missed payments, loan defaults, or credit card overdrafts, all of which lower a person's credit score. It is challenging to get new credit cards with poor credit scores, qualify for loans with attractive interest rates, or even find housing. Insurance rates and job chances that need a credit check may also be affected.

10. No Emergency Fund: People might not create an emergency fund if they don't have good money management skills. To cover unforeseen costs like medical bills, auto repairs, or lost income, you must have an emergency fund. Without this safety net, individuals could be compelled to rely on

high-interest loans or experience financial
disasters.

11. Increasing Dependence on Others for
Financial Assistance: Poor money
management might result in increasing
reliance on others for financial assistance.
Relationships may become strained, personal
liberty may be compromised, and
vulnerability may result. It can become
essential to rely on friends, family, or even
government help to satisfy basic
requirements.

12. Limited Access to Financial Possibilities:
Access to financial possibilities and
privileges may be impeded by poor money
management. For instance, those with a
history of poor money management may find
it challenging to get a mortgage, find a
desired rental, or get approved for a business
loan. A lack of financial prospects might

impede one's ability to advance personally and professionally.

13. Stress and Health Problems: Consistent financial mismanagement can lead to stress-related health problems. Anxiety, sadness, difficulty sleeping, and other physical and mental health issues have all been related to financial stress. The ongoing stress and ambiguity surrounding money can be detrimental to general well-being.

14. Missed Financial Goals: Individuals may find it difficult to reach their financial objectives without sound money management. Poor money management can hamper progress and postpone the accomplishment of desired goals, whether they are related to saving for a down payment on a home, starting a company, or paying for further education.

15. Limited Charity Contributions: Poor money management might limit a person's capacity to support charity organizations or give back to their society. Poor financial management may leave little opportunity for charity or supporting causes that are in line with one's values and views.

16. Deficient Financial Literacy: Poor money management might impede the acquisition of sound financial literacy techniques. People may continue a cycle of financial mismanagement and find it difficult to change their financial status if they don't understand the fundamentals of finance.

17. Lower Quality of Life: In the end, poor money management may result in a lower quality of life. The inability to satisfy personal and family demands, missed opportunities, and ongoing financial stress can all have a detrimental influence on

happiness, relationships, and general life satisfaction.

To prevent these effects and lay a firm financial foundation, it is crucial to establish excellent money management abilities. To recover control over their finances and attain long-term financial well-being, people might practice disciplined spending habits, develop a realistic budget, and seek out financial education.

Chapter 7

21 Proven Steps To Regain Financial Control

For long-term financial security and well-being, taking charge of your finances is crucial. Here are some practical methods of regaining financial control:

1. Create a Budget: Commence by putting together a thorough budget that details your earnings and outgoings. To better understand where your money is going, keep track of your expenditure and classify it. Set aside a certain amount each month for savings, debt reduction, and discretionary expenditures.

2. Track Your Expenses: Using a notepad, spreadsheet, or mobile application keep a log of all your outlays. This routine enables you to become more conscious of your spending

patterns, spot places where you may make savings, and adhere to your spending plan.

3. Reduce and Eliminate Debt: Create a strategy to systematically pay off your obligations. Pay the minimum on other obligations while concentrating on high-interest ones. Take into account debt consolidation or negotiating with creditors to minimize payments or interest rates. Limit your borrowing and put paying off your debts first.

4. Establish an Emergency Fund: Establish an emergency fund to cover unforeseen expenses such as vehicle repairs or unanticipated medical bills. Put up enough cash to last three to six months at your current level of living. Start small and increase your savings over time, if required.

5. Save and Invest: Establish savings objectives for both immediate and future needs. For each objective, like a down payment on a home, college costs, or retirement, set up a separate savings account. To increase your savings over time, consider investing in low-cost index funds or retirement accounts.

6. Prioritize Your Financial Goals: Identify Your Short-Term and Long-Term Financial Goals. Set priorities for your objectives and make financial decisions that are in line with them, whether they be retirement planning, debt repayment, or vacation savings. You may stay motivated and focused by doing this.

7. Reduce Expenses: Look for places where you might spend less money that is not essential. Analyze your spending habits to find non-essential goods and services you

may cut back on or go without. This can entail cutting back on entertainment, subscription services, or dining out costs.

8. Increase Your Income: Look at ways to raise your income. This may entail requesting a pay increase at work, accepting a side gig or freelancing employment, launching a side business, or investigating passive income sources. Increasing your income gives you more resources to achieve your financial objectives and speed up your debt reduction.

9. Seek Professional Advice: Think about speaking with a professional financial planner or financial advisor. They can offer advice on long-term financial planning, debt management, investments, and budgeting. Their knowledge may assist you in making wise choices and maximizing your financial plan.

10. Continue Your Education: Keep up your personal finance education. To increase your financial literacy, read books, articles, and trustworthy financial websites. To acquire the information and abilities needed to make better financial decisions, attend workshops or seminars.

11. Exercise Patience and Discipline: Managing your finances demands patience and discipline. Maintain consistency in your spending, savings, and debt-repayment strategy. Maintain your dedication to your financial objectives and refrain from rash purchases.

12. Negotiate your recurrent costs, such as utility bills, insurance, and subscriptions. Speak with service providers and bargain for lower prices, or explore cost-effective alternatives. Do not be hesitant to inquire about discounts or compare prices.

13. Automate Savings: Set up recurring deductions from your checking account for investments or savings. With less reliance on willpower, this makes sure that you regularly save money. To put your financial objectives first, see saving as a non-negotiable expenditure.

14. Monitor Your Net Worth: Determine your net worth regularly by deducting your obligations from your assets (savings, investments, and real estate). You can track your progress and assess the overall improvement of your financial condition by keeping track of your net worth over time.

15. Avoid Impulse Buys: Spend money carefully before making any purchases, especially for non-essential products. Take a moment to consider whether the purchase fits with your beliefs, is within your price range,

and advances your long-term objectives. Delaying gratification might reduce impulsive buying.

16. Review Insurance Coverage: Make sure your insurance plans offer sufficient protection at fair prices by routinely reviewing them. Look around for better choices and take into account bundling insurance for potential savings. This minimizes expenditures while assisting in asset protection.

17. Pay Attention to Financial Education: Keep learning about personal finance-related subjects. To increase your financial literacy, enroll in online classes, webinars, or workshops. You can make better selections if you are familiar with ideas like investing, retirement planning, and tax techniques.

18. Regularly Review and Adjust: Spend some time occasionally reviewing your financial status. Evaluate your progress toward your objectives, spot any areas that need improvement, and make the required changes. It's critical to modify your financial strategy when your financial situation changes.

19. Embrace a thrifty attitude by looking for methods to decrease costs and save money without compromising your quality of life. Search for deals, use coupons, purchase during sales, and think about purchasing used or reconditioned things. Over time, even small saves may add up.

20. Include Your Family: If appropriate, include your family in the management of your funds. Talk about your financial objectives as a couple, make decisions together, and develop a common appreciation

for the significance of sound financial management. Everyone can stay on track by having a pen dialogue regarding money. Review your credit card, bank, and investment account statements regularly

21. Review Your Financial Statements. This enables you to see any mistakes, spot any unapproved transactions, and maintain awareness of your financial operations.

Keep in mind that taking charge of your finances is a process that calls for dedication, self-control, and continual work. It's important to be flexible, ask for help when you need it, and continually assess and improve your financial approach as your situation changes.

Chapter 8

Living Within Your Means

To "live within your means" is to control your spending and lifestyle such that it doesn't surpass your income or financial resources. It entails choosing wisely and sustainably from your available resources without taking on excessive debt or depending on unsustainable financial habits.

Key components of living within your means include the following:

1. Budgeting: One of the key components of living within your means is making a budget. It entails identifying every source of revenue you have and classifying your outgoing costs. You may make sure that you don't overspend and that your costs match your income by keeping track of what

you spend and exercising control over
it.

2. Avoiding debt traps: While certain
    debt, such as a mortgage or a suitable
    school loan, may be appropriate, living
    within your means necessitates staying
    away from high-interest loans that may
    easily spiral out of control. It can be
    difficult to keep a healthy financial life
    when you have a lot of high-interest
    debt from credit card debt, payday
    loans, or excessive personal loans.

3. Emergency cash reserves: To deal with
    unforeseen costs or a brief lack of
    income, you must build an emergency
    fund. When confronted with
    unanticipated situations, such as
    medical problems or job layoffs, this
    safety net can help you avoid going
    into debt.

4. Prioritization and cost-cutting: Making deliberate decisions about your expenditures is frequently a part of living within your means. It could entail choosing to live frugally and prioritizing needs over wants to save money.

5. Financial long-term planning: To guarantee that you can maintain your lifestyle beyond the present, planning for the future is essential. This includes creating financial objectives, making sensible investments, and saving for retirement.

6. Dispensing with comparison: Comparing your lifestyle or assets to others is a common pitfall that can cause you to overspend or make poor financial decisions. Focusing on your

financial circumstances and aspirations rather than attempting to live up to someone else's standard of life is necessary to live within your means.

Living within your means offers financial security and mental tranquility. It enables you to keep control of your money, lessen financial stress, and work toward attaining your long-term financial goals.

How should you live within your means?

Living within your means involves persistence, patience, and resolve. However, I want you to take into account the following guidance that will help you get there.

1. Establish a budget: Begin by evaluating your earnings and outgoing costs. Identify your monthly income, fixed costs (rent,

utilities, loan payments), variable expenses (groceries, entertainment), and savings targets. Keep to your spending plan and evaluate it frequently.

2. Track your spending: Keep a record of every penny you spend. This makes it easier for you to see where your money is going and gives you the ability to make the necessary adjustments to match your spending to your income.

3. Set your necessities and wants apart and prioritize your needs. Prioritize taking care of your basic requirements, including those for food, shelter, utilities, and healthcare. Before covering your basic costs, keep your discretionary spending to a minimum.

4. Cut back on discretionary spending: Consider your spending patterns and seek places where you may make savings. This

can entail cutting back on eating out, lowering entertainment costs, or locating more affordable options for particular goods or services.

5. Manage debt properly or avoid it: Debt can cause financial misery very rapidly. Reduce your reliance on credit cards and loans. Make a strategy to progressively pay off your debts, starting with the ones with the highest interest rates, if you have any.

6. Save frequently: Give saving a high priority in your spending plan. A percentage of your income should be set away for retirement, plans, and emergency savings. Set up automatic transfers from your checking to your savings accounts to automate your savings.

7. Comparison shop: Check for sales or discounts while purchasing purchases and

compare prices. If it makes more financial sense to do so, think about borrowing or purchasing old goods.

8. Prepare meals at home: Since eating out might be expensive, try to prepare as many of your meals at home as you can. You have better control over the caliber of the materials and your health, in addition to it being more cost-effective.

9. Engage in thoughtful spending: Think twice before purchasing to be sure it meets your requirements and financial objectives. Avoid making impulsive purchases and allow yourself time to decide if the purchase is required or unnecessary.

10. Invest in your financial education: Learn about investing, budgeting, and personal finance. You'll be better able to manage your

money and make wise financial decisions if you comprehend these ideas.

11. Set appropriate financial goals. Identify your short- and long-term financial goals. This might involve settling debt, establishing an emergency fund, or laying aside money for a down payment on a house. Setting realistic goals will help you stay motivated and committed to living within your means.

12. Avoid lifestyle inflation: Refrain from expanding your lifestyle proportionately as your income rises. Instead, retain or expand your investments and savings while limiting your spending.

13. Pay using cash or debit cards: Using cash or debit cards might help you keep your expenditures within your allocated budget. This lowers the chance of racking up credit card debt and promotes fiscal responsibility.

14. Bargain and look for discounts: When making significant purchases or signing up for services, don't be afraid to bargain for lower pricing or look for deals. You might be able to negotiate a cheaper price with many suppliers by just asking.

15. Look for free or inexpensive substitutes: Look for inexpensive substitutes for the activities and services you like. Think about viewing a movie at home or going to free events and festivals in your neighborhood as an alternative to going to the theaters.

16. Embrace delayed satisfaction: Embrace delayed gratification rather than acting on impulse. Wait for a certain amount of time (such as 24 hours or a week) after discovering something you like before making a purchase. The urge frequently

disappears, allowing you to choose
something based on logic.

17. Create an emergency fund: Financial
stability depends on having an emergency
reserve. In case of unforeseen circumstances,
such as job loss or medical difficulties, try to
save at least three to six months' worth of
living costs.

18. Avoid paying for unneeded subscriptions:
Review your services and think about
deleting those you seldom use or don't need.
To cut any unneeded costs, review your
subscriptions to streaming services, gyms,
magazines, and other regular charges.

19. Adopt a thrifty lifestyle: Adopt practices
include shopping at secondhand stores,
utilizing coupons, mending objects rather
than replacing them, and looking for free or
inexpensive entertainment choices.

20. Surround yourself with people who share your views: Associate with others who share your dedication to living within your means and who have comparable financial goals. Their behaviors and outlook on life can help and strengthen your financial self-discipline.

Keep in mind that living within your means doesn't imply depriving yourself; rather, it means making decisions consciously that are in line with your financial being. You may increase your financial stability and have a more secure future by using these tips and keeping a positive outlook.

Chapter 9

Increasing financial competence and knowledge

Making wise financial decisions, handling money well, and attaining long-term financial objectives all depend on having better financial literacy and abilities. The following actions can help you improve your financial literacy:

1. Educate Yourself: Begin by reading books, articles, and trustworthy websites on personal finance-related subjects. Study financial topics such as debt management, retirement planning, investing, and budgeting. Learn the terms and ideas used in the financial industry.

2. Attend Online Workshops or Courses: Numerous websites and educational organizations provide workshops and courses on personal finance and investment. Enroll in

classes that support your educational objectives and offer organized instruction on a range of financial subjects. You may enhance your knowledge and acquire useful skills with these courses.

3. Read Financial Professionals' Blogs and Podcasts: Read the blogs and podcasts of recognized financial professionals who offer advice on personal money. You may learn various viewpoints, tactics, and best practices for handling your money by regularly reading their articles.

4. Attend Financial Workshops or Seminars: Look for local financial management or personal finance workshops in your area. These occasions frequently offer helpful information, resources, and techniques for enhancing your financial knowledge. Utilize all chances you have to go to such activities in your neighborhood.

5. Use Online Resources and Tools: To improve your money management abilities, make use of Internet financial tools and services. To get experience monitoring spending, establishing financial goals, and managing your finances, use budgeting applications, online calculators, investment trackers, and other digital resources.

6. Seek Expert Advice: Think about speaking with a financial advisor or a certified financial planner. Based on your particular financial objectives and circumstances, they may offer tailored advice, assist you in developing a financial strategy, and direct you in making wise decisions.

7. Develop a budget and stick to it to keep tabs on your earnings, outgoing costs, and savings. Review your spending patterns about your budget regularly and make

necessary improvements. Making deliberate financial decisions, establishing priorities, and developing discipline are all made easier with a budget.

8. Gain an Understanding of Investments: Acquire a working knowledge of the fundamentals of investing, including stocks, bonds, mutual funds, and retirement accounts. Discover how to allocate your assets, determine your risk tolerance, and develop long-term investment plans. Start modestly and steadily grow your knowledge and portfolio over time.

9. Effective Debt Management: Become knowledgeable about the various debt categories, interest rates, and repayment options. Discover ways to consolidate debt, choose a refinancing strategy, and accelerate your debt repayment. Understanding debt management enables you to avoid taking on

excessive debt, reduce interest costs, and keep your finances stable.

10. Keep-Up-To-Date on Taxes: Become familiar with the tax rules and guidelines that apply to your nation or region. Recognize how certain financial decisions, such as investments, retirement accounts, and deductions, may affect your taxes. Keep abreast of any tax law amendments that may affect your financial status.

11. Build a Network and Share Knowledge: Interact with people who share your interest in personal finance. Participate in financial communities, go to financial meetings, or join online forums. Sharing information and experiences may lead to the development of fresh viewpoints, ideas, and money management advice.

Keep in mind that gaining financial literacy is a lifelong endeavor. Always look for ways to learn more, keep up with current events in finance, and modify your abilities when your financial position changes. You may build confidence, make wise decisions, and move toward attaining your financial objectives by devoting time and effort to enhancing your financial literacy.

Chapter 10

Methods for creating solid financial habits

For long-term financial stability, it is crucial to cultivate sound financial practices. Here are some crucial actions you may take to establish and uphold sound financial practices:

1. Establish explicit financial objectives: Set clear and explicit financial objectives as your first step. Having clearly defined objectives may help give your financial habits focus and drive, whether it's saving for a down payment on a home, paying off debt, or creating an emergency fund.

2. Establish a realistic budget: Create a budget that supports your financial objectives. Keep track of your income and costs, classify your purchases, and assign

exact sums to each category. Be honest with yourself about your income and outgoing costs, and make sure your budget is long-term-sustainable.

3. Automate bill payments and savings: Set up automatic deductions from your paycheck for investments or savings accounts. This makes it easier for you to regularly save money and lessens the urge to spend it. Automate your bill payments as well to guarantee that they are made on time and avoid incurring late fees and penalties.

4. Track your spending: To know where your money is going, keep a log of your outgoing costs. Track your expenditures with a spreadsheet, a smartphone app, or an internet tool. Review your spending patterns frequently to see areas where you may make changes to better fit your budget and financial objectives.

5. Make debt repayment a priority: If you have debt, make it a point to repay it over time. Pay the minimum on other obligations while concentrating on high-interest ones. Think about debt-reduction techniques like the debt-avalanche or debt-snowball approach. Over time, your financial situation might be improved by steadily paying down debt.

6. Practice living within your means by keeping your expenses below your income. Avert excessive lifestyle inflation and the need to imitate other people's spending patterns. Instead of focusing on material goods, concentrate on finding happiness and pleasure in relationships and experiences.

7. Create an emergency reserve: Create a reserve for unforeseen costs or financial losses. Try to save enough money for three to

six months of expenses. Start by routinely setting aside little sums, then progressively raise them as time goes on.

8. Avoid impulsive purchases: Follow the 24-hour rule before making a purchase, especially of non-essential things. Spend a day deciding whether the purchase fits your requirements and financial objectives. Make thoughtful financial judgments rather than acting on impulse.

9. Keep learning: Commit to continued financial education. Learn about personal finance through reading books, articles, and blogs. Keep up on pertinent financial trends, investing methods, and news. You'll be more prepared to make wise financial decisions the more information you possess.

10. Develop the practice of delayed gratification: Develop the practice of

delaying short-term desires in favor of long-term financial objectives. Give yourself time to consider if a purchase is in line with your beliefs and priorities before buying it to avoid making impulsive purchases.

11. Routinely review and reflect: Make time to routinely review and reflect on your financial objectives, habits, and progress, such as monthly or quarterly. Celebrate your successes and milestones, and make necessary changes to your routines and tactics.

12. Surround yourself with positive influences: Spend time with people who have sound money management practices and optimistic financial outlooks. Ask friends, family, or financial networks that encourage sensible financial practices for help and responsibility.

Keep in mind that developing sound financial practices is an ongoing effort. It necessitates self-control, endurance, and alertness. You may create a solid foundation for financial security and realize your long-term financial objectives by continually putting these behaviors into practice.

Chapter 11

Strategies for overcoming financial mismanagement

Financial mismanagement must be overcome with a proactive strategy and a dedication to transformation. The following are some tips to assist you overcome poor money management:

1. Acknowledge and Evaluate the Situation: Admit that your money management is flawed and accept responsibility for it. By analyzing your existing financial condition, debts, and spending patterns, you can determine the severity of the problem. Having a clear understanding of the problem's breadth is essential for creating a strategy.

2. Establish a Realistic Budget: Make a thorough budget that precisely reflects your

earnings, outgoings, and financial objectives. Regarding your income and spending, be honest, and allocate money as necessary. To keep track of your expenditures and make sure you stick to your budget, think about utilizing budgeting apps or spreadsheets.

3. Prioritize Debt Repayment: Create a strategy to methodically pay off your obligations. Make minimum payments on other obligations while putting high-interest loans first. Investigate debt-paying techniques like the debt avalanche or debt snowball approach. If you need help putting together an efficient debt repayment strategy, think about consulting an expert.

4. Reduce Expenses: Look for places where you may save money and stop spending on necessary things. Examine your spending patterns and cut back on or eliminate discretionary expenditures. On bills,

subscriptions, eating out, and entertainment, look for methods to save costs. Every dollar saved might be used for savings or debt reduction.

5. Create an Emergency Fund: Create an emergency fund to pay for unforeseen costs and monetary losses. Increase your savings contributions gradually after beginning with tiny regular installments. A financial safety net is created by having an emergency reserve, which eliminates the need to use credit cards or take out loans to cover unforeseen bills.

6. Seek Professional Advice: Take into consideration speaking with a financial adviser or a credit counselor. They may provide you with professional advice, assist you in putting together a financial strategy, and offer tips for overcoming financial mismanagement. Additionally, based on your

unique situation, they may provide you with individualized recommendations.

7. Boost Financial Literacy: Spend money on your financial education by reading books, going to workshops, or enrolling in online courses on personal finance. You'll be better able to make wise judgments, improve your money management abilities, and stay away from frequent financial dangers if you increase your financial literacy.

8. Set Realistic Goals: Set realistic financial objectives. Set short-term objectives to get going and boost your confidence. As you advance, increase the scope of your long-term objectives. Review your objectives frequently, monitor your development, and recognize accomplishments as they happen.

9. Be Responsive and Seek Support: Tell a trustworthy friend or relative who can hold

you accountable about your financial objectives and how you're doing. Consider participating in online forums or communities where you might meet people who are also trying to improve their financial status. Support and inspiration may be gained by discussing struggles and experiences.

10. Put Patience and Persistence into Practice: Overcoming financial mismanagement is a path that calls for both of these qualities. Recognize that things will need time to change. Maintain your dedication to your financial strategy, practice restraint with your spending and saving, and show patience as you advance.

To overcome financial mismanagement, keep in mind that it takes time, persistent work, and the commitment to break bad patterns. You may reclaim control of your money and lay a strong foundation for a healthy financial future by putting these techniques into practice and remaining dedicated to developing your financial management abilities.

Chapter 12

How to sustain long-term prosperity and financial stability?

It takes perseverance, self-control, and a proactive mindset to maintain financial wellness and long-term success. Here are some tactics to support your continued financial stability and your long-term success:

1. Continuously examine and update your financial plan: This includes your budget, financial objectives, and investing strategy. As you reach key objectives, evaluate your progress, make the appropriate changes, and establish new objectives. Keep your financial plan current to make sure it reflects your changing goals and requirements.

2. Give saving and investing priority: Consistently give saving and investing

priority. Maintain your regular savings habits and contributions to your retirement accounts. As your income increases or when you have more money available, increase your savings. Keep abreast of investing possibilities and tweak your investment plan as necessary.

3. Manage your debt sensibly: Avoid needless borrowing and pay off current obligations methodically to manage your debt sensibly. Reduce your high-interest debt as much as possible, and plan out your debt payback strategy. If you want to lower your interest rates or combine several loans into one loan with better conditions, look into refinancing possibilities.

4. Create and maintain an emergency fund: Continue to give the creation and maintenance of an emergent priority. Three to six months' worth of costs for a living should

be saved in this fund. Regularly check the status of your emergency fund and add to it if necessary to cover unforeseen costs.

5. Keep track of your expenses: Continue to monitor and assess your outgoing costs to make sure they complement your spending plan and monetary objectives. Analyze your spending habits frequently, look for places where you may minimize costs, and keep an eye on your discretionary spending. Look for ways to save costs on ongoing expenses or bargain for lower service costs.

6. Maintain healthy financial habits: Consistently engage in healthy financial practices. This entails handling your financial affairs carefully and paying your obligations on time as well as routinely checking your credit report. Refrain from making impulsive purchases, engage in delayed gratification,

and focus your financial decisions on your long-term objectives.

7. Continue your education and informedness: Continue your financial education. Keep abreast of adjustments to tax rules, investment possibilities, and market developments. To increase your knowledge and keep current with best practices, read books, go to seminars or webinars, and follow reliable financial resources.

8. Seek professional advice: Take into account routinely speaking with a financial planner or advisor. They may give advice, assist you in evaluating your financial situation, and offer perceptions of investing tactics or retirement planning. A professional can assist you manage difficult financial issues and offer insightful advice.

9. Safeguard your assets and manage risks: Consistently assess your insurance coverage to make sure it effectively safeguards your assets and reduces risks. Update insurance as necessary, and depending on your situation, think about adding more coverage. Make sure your estate planning papers, such as trusts or wills, represent your current intentions by reviewing them.

10. Develop a positive attitude: Keep an optimistic and proactive attitude about your financial path. Celebrate your successes, keep inspired, and maintain your fortitude in the face of financial difficulties. Have faith in your capacity for long-term financial success and work tirelessly to attain it.

Keep in mind that achieving long-term success and well-being is a lifelong endeavor. Assess your progress frequently, make adjustments to your plans as necessary, and

maintain your dedication to your financial
security. You may retain financial stability
and strive toward a wealthy future by
implementing these tactics and making
thoughtful financial decisions.

Conclusion

I hope that by the time you reach the end of this book, you will have gained insightful knowledge, useful advice, and a renewed sense of authority over your financial situation. One of the most important steps in achieving financial freedom and stability is realizing and correcting the basic faults that frequently cause our financial journeys to fail.

Do not forget that handling your funds is a lifelong responsibility rather than a one-time event. It demands self-control, introspection, and a willingness to change. By applying the principles you've learned in these pages, you may change your relationship with money and lay the groundwork for a more productive financial future.

Establish a sensible budget, keep careful tabs on your spending, and give saving for

long-term objectives and emergencies
priority. Make a concerted effort to cut back
on wasteful spending and recognize the
difference between needs and wants. Learn
about investing, diversify your holdings, and
when required, seek expert guidance.
Develop sound financial practices that are
consistent with your beliefs and objectives,
and are most essential.

Recognize that obstacles could appear along
the road. We all face unforeseen difficulties
since financial paths are rarely linear. But
with the information and skills you've learned
from this book, you can overcome these
challenges with assurance and resiliency.

Beyond the figures on a balance sheet,
financial wellness includes the independence
and peace of mind that come with being in
charge of your financial future. It enables you
to achieve your goals, care for your loved

ones, and have a beneficial influence on your neighborhood.

Commit to acting when you finish reading this book. Apply your new knowledge unattempted to develop sound financial practices in your daily life. Accept the road of personal development and financial empowerment, and keep in mind that regular tiny actions can add up to major advancement over time.

And last, take note that you are not alone. Ask for help from family members, financial planners, and groups of like-minded people who can offer direction, encouragement, and accountability. Together, we can build a society where everyone has access to financial security.

Thank you for starting the process of improving your financial situation. May you find this book to be a helpful tool on your road to financial success, and may your newfound wisdom and resolve help you get closer to the abundant and secure life you so richly deserve.

Here's to a future brimming with financial freedom, mental tranquility, and countless opportunities. Cheers to your quest toward financial mastery and creating a prosperous life!